Absinthe and Oatmeal

Absinthe and Oatmeal

A poetry collection

Ginny Grush

NEW ALEXANDRIA PRESS
LIVONIA

Published by New Alexandria Press
PO Box 530516
Livonia, Michigan 48153
www.newalexandriapress.com

This book is a work of fiction. Any names, characters, and events portrayed in this book are entirely fictitious, and are the product of the author's imagination. Any resemblance to any actual person–living, dead, or otherwise–is entirely coincidental.

Cover design ©2016 by Jonathan Higgins

Softcover Edition:
ISBN-10: 1-60916-027-9
ISBN-13: 978-1-60915-027-3

Quantity discounts are available on bulk purchases of this book Special books or book excerpts can also be made available to fit specific needs. For information, please contact sales@newalexandriapress.com or send written inquiries to New Alexandria Press, PO Box 530516, Livonia, Michigan 48153.

Printed in the United States of America

10 9 8 7 6 5 4 3 2 1

For Ernie, Cindy, Andy, Carlos, and Vincent....

Contents

IV Nature and Here and There

V Rants and Rhymes

And...worse...become a poet, which they say is an incurable and infectious disease....

—Miguel de Cervantes

Don Quixote

I
Out of Detroit

Fast Times at Euclid Beach

How good they felt
those heart-grabbing, gut-churning
head-knocking, butt-thumping
amusement park rides.
Back when nothing could go too fast.
Our parents on benches, not far away
praying for a whiff of cool lake breeze.
We kids all damp and sticky
headed moth-like for the thrills.
Seduced by speed and daring
how we could hardly wait
to feel stomachs suspended
as the Cyclone crested the hill
to be wave-slapped into drenching
at the bottom of the Old Mill Race
to be plastered to our seat backs
as the Tilt-a-Whirl rose and fell
to ram each other silly
in the Dodgem's theater of war.
For all those spins, jerks, lurches
and death-defying drops
we could hardly wait.
And how good it felt
back when nothing could go too fast.

Why So Shy?

Just born this way
not wanting attention.
An only child
I kept my own counsel
had imaginary friends.

Loved school but
really didn't have anything to say.
Answered only when called on.
Knew I didn't know that much.
Just wanted to listen and read.
Got in trouble for reading during math.

Couldn't understand
kids who cried
in front of the class
or jumped up and down
yelling, Me, teacher, me!
Never liked Art Linkletter for
embarrassing little kids on TV.

Besides, I had eyes in my head.
No Shirley Temple, I'd figured out why
I was a farmer—not a flower
in the dance recital.
And though I loved piano
couldn't keep my knees
from knocking,
my fingers from freezing in recitals.

But finally, because I felt bad for
my poor mother always hearing
"*She never says anything*"—
and because they shamed me,
testing me for speech defects,
figuring I guess, I couldn't speak at all—
finally, I started to try to change.

Sign of the Past

Nine years old
in the car with Mom and Dad
heading south
for our big Florida vacation.
Reading crisp white letters
painted on brick-red barns.
Falling for the come-on for a "chaw."

CHEW MAIL POUCH TOBACCO

"Mom, I saw the Louisiana license first.
Who chews tobacco, anyway?
Yuck, and they just spit it out?
And it gives them cancer?
How far to Gatlinburg, now, Daddy?
Why can't I sing Ninety-nine Bottles of Beer?
Will I have to eat grits too?
Hey, there's another barn."

CHEW MAIL POUCH TOBACCO

Burned into my brain back then
those four compelling words.
and I made a vow
that someday I would try some.

Now, I read the last sign's painted
the very last painter retired
the old ads to grow ghostly, worn and faded.
Still their message I remember,
and I pledge that someday yet—I'll buy and

CHEW some MAIL POUCH TOBACCO

Soldiers for a Day
A Kid's Science Lesson

The Rainbow Diner on Lake Erie
halfway to Cleveland from Detroit.
Lunch stop on summer car trips
back to the relatives.
And always, always—its white wood exterior
and all its window screens covered
with the light brown, brittle remains
of that year's attack of Canadian Soldiers.
Hundreds of them.

The fish flies' icky carcasses
way more interesting to me than
Perry's Monument out on Put-In-Bay island
with its lake history mom would tell.
More intriguing by far
than the counter-sized slot machines
inside the eatery dad wouldn't let me play.

Made me go to the library
where I found that the Soldiers' assault
is mouthless, messy and short,
the hatch exploding from the lake
with one day to live, propagate
and then—die.

Unmoved by the sad shortness
or one-purposed-ness of their lives,
I was delighted to learn further
that the Soldiers add collateral damage
when their carcasses pile high
and deep enough to become
a crunchy, slippery, fish-mealy road hazard.

What THEM Gave Me

First, that sound
that piercing, high-pitched
pulsating, unforgettable E-E-E-E.
Then, huge purple letters against
the movie's black-and-white
spelling out the title—THEM.
Shortly, from back of a dune
two hairy antennae, big bug eyes
pincers opening and closing and
a giant ant, lunging for the girl scientist.
Broke the strap on my sundress
jumping out of my seat.
Didn't care because
I was in love with—being scared.
THEM it was made me a horror fan.

THEM taught me stuff, too.
Like ants kill by sting of formic acid
and ant in Latin is formica.
And we'd better not mess around
with that nuclear testing thing
Lest we unleash a horror of biblical proportions.

Best of all THEM gave me
a heroine smart, feisty and fearless

a woman who knew her ants.
Right with the guys
she rappels into the nest,
test-licks the goo on the walls,
photographs the queen's chamber,
then orders the men—to blast the eggs.

Thrills, nuggets of knowledge, philosophy
bad grammar and nascent feminism.
Not bad for a fifties B-movie.

Christmas Tree Remembered

The pine smell surrounds us
as we suffer pricks and blotches
of dark, sticky stuff
until the tree is positioned
just right.

The glowing strings of lights
that we test
cast colored circles on the rug.
By unanimous choice
no white bulbs are allowed.

Our very "specialist" string
with the red and gold tubes of oil,
Daddy hooks on straight and secure,
so the bubbles rise furiously,
gloriously.

The ornaments we hang
with care and practicality,
the biggest in the large spots
the littlest near the top.

Treasured breakables
Mama treats with such tender care
that the delicate blue glass butterfly
and golden goose
last to another generation.

All the handmades and uglies
we give low-down
in-the-back placement.

And since our angel
is just a pretty face,
a design stamped on paper
and pasted to a circle
of white fiber glass,
we make her a beauty
by bathing her in a halo
of blue light.

Patiently, we separate the tinsel.
Reverently, we place each strand
to dangle free and shimmer.
Finished, we enjoy the vision
standing right in front,
looking long and hard.

But, I alone, know
the three very best spots
to view our tree.
First, halfway down the stairs
in the corner by the tree,
leaning over the banister
and gazing down
with color, light and green
spreading out below me
as if I were the angel on top.

Then, over by the fireplace,
looking into the mantel mirror,
the round, convex, gold-framed one
with an eagle on top,
where I see our tree's reflection,
all chunky and compressed
and imagine the mirror to be
a porthole to another world,
one that I might enter
some magic Christmas Eve.

But best of all,
both fantastic and forbidden,
is the view I enjoy only on the sneak.
When, lying on my back
on the floor, I wiggle myself in
as far as I can get
right under the tree
to look up through
its tiers and layers of branches,
and breathe the beauty in.

My Words-in-Waiting

At twelve I tried "uncouth"
on one of the neighborhood boys
as in "Don't be *uncouth*."

"*Ungoose?*" he repeated
shoving me away
to get on with kick-the-can.
Not a good tease or flirt word
for that pre-pubescent time.

So, I learned to wait to use
the words I loved.
Lugubrious, malodorous, elephantine
bogus and mesmerized
all needed their perfect moments.
Aspidistra, asafetida
and legerdemain as well.

It took years—but finally,
defending Michigan's
record-breaking fungus
against a Washington state pretender,
I got to rebut and even pun on
the defamers—calling out
their "morel turpitude."

Cellar door,
someone once told me,
is the most beautiful-sounding
pair of words in the English language.
Can't disagree.
But what to do with them?
A song or poem about how to
Sell a Door to Stella D'Oro?

Place names I hold dear
await their chronicling.
No one should not hear of
Twisp, Monkey's Eyebrow,
Buzzard Acres, Dismal Hollow,
Omps, Cacapon or Snake Eyes.

Say, wanna hear about the time I was in ….

Childhood's End

That year we got a piano
and I started lessons.
Dad got three weeks vacation
and we drove to Florida.
We remodeled the kitchen
and Mom got the first dishwasher
on our street.
I saw my still-favorite scary movie—THEM.

In November, at ten-and-a-half,
I made my Confirmation.
The Bishop dabbed holy oil
on my forehead and gave me a slap,
hardening me to become a soldier of Christ.
Only a tap, but my folks were watching and I felt
grown up, a fighter for Jesus if need be.
Didn't know who I'd fight in northwest Detroit.

The morning after Thanksgiving
I watched Dad go down the street to the bus stop
his funny up-down, up-down walk
the same as mine.
I had no school and Mom had the car for errands.

I was in the front yard when Uncle came
looking for Mom—not saying why.
She pulled in and he hurried her inside
left me standing in the driveway
fingering the portholes on our Buick.
Her cry came right through the door.

At the funeral home I wondered how
a bouquet of little pink roses
with DADDY pasted on in gold letters
got placed inside the casket.
No-one had asked me.

Dynasty of One

I am a first, last and only Ames.
No tie to the founders of Ames, Iowa
nor the AMES lawn implements company
though husband jokes
he was misinformed I was their heiress.
I'm not related to Ed
who's not an Ames either
but a singer of Ukrainian-Jewish descent
who played an Indian on TV.

No, dad just tired of
spelling and pronouncing
his Bohemian surname, Zamecnik
and of being last on every list.
So, he lopped off the z
dropped the nik, changed c to s
made it Ames and made it legal.
I always liked it,
its sound and simplicity.
Mom, dad and I were a happy clan.
Though that first in the alphabet thing
meant my sitting up front in every class
and being called on first.

* * * * *

Dad died and left us two.
Mom died and left me one
carrying on the name through college
and Peace Corps—where
the good folks of rural Bolivia
found it strange, a bit hard to say
and thus pronounced it AH-mess.

All in all, it was a good reign.

Candy Poor
A Detroit Halloween

Our cry echoed
up, down and across St. Mary's
bouncing from one house to another
all with their porch lights on.
A plaintive, demanding, urgent
"Help the Poor."

Greedy little beggars we were
the gang from the first block
south of Seven Mile.
Out for candy—all we could get
figuring we were the poor of that plea.
Running up steps, bags opened wide,
mumbling *"Thanks"* so fast
the neighbors hardly saw us
or the costumes we were wearing.

Lots of kids back then
with lots of blocks of lots of houses to hit.
Word passed as to where popcorn balls
and chocolate bars could be found
and the house handing out ice creams.
Not much time, never enough time
for us to *"Help the Poor."*

II

Absinthe and Oatmeal

Eponymous

Look, they're named for you
"For-Cynthias."
Or so I told my toddler
Cindy, long ago.
So, now, for me—for always
those small, bright, yellow
harbingers of spring
can have no other name.

Doña Berta

She shakes her head.
Dark curls bob in disbelief.
Black eyes smile
as we compare hands.
Four palms
outstretched and upturned.
Hers, nut-brown and calloused
mine, soft, smooth and white.
The difference makes us laugh.

She continues grinding corn,
standing by the hollowed *tacú* stump
pressing down with the *mano* stick,
turning, lifting, pressing again.

I've arrived in Palometillas
to worry about the water, the latrines
the nearby school—empty of books.

She calls me *pobrecita*
for coming so far
for leaving my country
for my mother being dead.
I call her *valiente*
for the *chaco* farm she runs
for the children she's borne
the six who lived
and the eight who died.

I wonder at how hard it is
to cook by fire
haul water up the well,
bathe in the river
iron with hot coals.
She wonders at
my clothes of polyester
my underwear and shoes
my lack of missing teeth,
and the odd way I drink my coffee
big and black.

Velorio

I rode to Yolanda's wake
in the tractor-drawn cart
that brought her casket.
Don Julio drove and I held on in back
as we bumped the two miles in
on an old, rutted oxcart trail.
The rest of the Coca-Salazares walked
and made nearly as good time.
I'd never been to a velorio
and hardly knew Yolanda.

We'd exchanged a few words once
as she sat waiting for the bus to Santa Cruz
in front of Doña Berta's.
Young, pretty, smiling, but dressed *de luto*,
Yolanda was pleasant, polite, amused by my accent.
The mourning clothes were for her mother,
dead now, about a year, she told me,
then confided she was pregnant again,
with her fifth and on her way in to the doctor.

Arriving at the *chaco*, the tractor pulled up
to its white-walled, thatched-roof farmhouse.
A crowd had already gathered.
Inside, Yolanda lay on a mahogany door,
the front door of her house,
taken down for this sad purpose
and balanced between two benches.

Hibiscus, poinsettias, birds-of-paradise
and lighted, white candles surrounded her body.
People cried, moaned and wailed.
I prayed with them at her side.

Yolanda had died giving birth,
the infant now in the care of the *comadre*.
*"A woman shouldn't have that many children
one after another,"* Berta whispered to me.
*"I was blessed—surviving my fourteen childbirths
and losing only eight of the babies."*

Change of Season

Once I lived where
there was year-round green.
Hot, living, breathing
jungle vegetation green
And bougainvillea, birds-of-paradise
hibiscus and poinsettias.
Fat-trunked pink *toborochis*
and tall red *cosorios*.
Growth so fast, so dense
land was cleared by fire and machete.

Hot and humid or hot and dry
with occasional cold rains from the south.
Sweat rolled off you at midday
dropped you into a stupor
for the *hora de siesta*.
Respite came at night, sitting outside
on a packed-earth clearing
swatting mosquitoes and looking up
at a huge, black dome of sky
punctuated with thousands of stars.
No Polaris—no Big Dipper
but, low, near the horizon—the Southern Cross.

I acclimated, became a *camba boliviana*
for my two years.
Might have stayed if there'd been a job
or there'd been a person.
Yet, if I had, my Midwestern soul
would always have missed one thing:
Autumn—with its turning of the leaves
from green to the oranges, reds and golds
of firefalls cascading from the trees.

Absinthe

I pour half a cup of ice-cold water
down slowly over the sugar cube
I've placed on a slotted spoon
above my birthday absinthe.
And the clear, aromatic liquid
waiting in the bottom of my glass
louches as promised
turning cloudy and pale green.

*"Lovely, that opalescent chartreuse
and its aroma of anise,"* I say to
my dear enablers
the pair who searched long
for a bottle for me—
ever since I read real absinthe
was being made again.
"Mucousy with a smell of cat urine," says husband.
"Snot-like, odor of Black Jack gum," adds son.
They do not share my passion.

I sip.
Strange. Wonderful. Unforgettable.
"*Liquid licorice,*" I say
to a now empty kitchen.
I continue alone—imbibing The Green Fairy.
THE drink of Bohemian Paris.
Of the dissolute, dissipated, dopey-looking
depressed subjects of Lautrec, Van Gogh, Picasso
guys who themselves got drunk on the stuff.

I wait
for inspiration, voices, visions
madness, paralysis
an urge to cut off my ear.

Nothing.
I guess the modern formula
did neutralize the wormwood's bad effects.
I am experiencing quite a nice buzz though.

At the Old Absinthe House
on our honeymoon in New Orleans,
the waitress warned me against their specialty.
"You might not like it, Sweetie, it tastes like licorice."

Me?—the lover of black jelly beans, Black Crows
Sen-Sen and tarragon.
I ordered one right away.
Ah! The romance of that time.
The decadence of the setting.

But later I learned REAL absinthe
had long been banned
for problems like rotting out people's brains.
What I'd tried was only anisette.
I vowed to get me the real thing.

And so, a decades-long search began
and now it ends—in satisfaction
satisfaction and the world's greatest aftertaste.

Quick, Quick

Halting, teasing, timid and late
this year's Michigan spring,
waiting for the melt of the pocked, grainy
little glacial ridges of plowed snow.
On its heels—summer erupts.

My forsythia refuse to bloom.
My lilacs burst open so fast
their perfume competes with
the aphrodisia of the apple blossoms.
Robins, hustling and scurrying to nest
choose a spot right by our front door
squawking every time we open it.

Husband and I walk the circle of our sub.
"Originals" here, we've known
these trees, flowers and shrubs
since their plantings, years ago.
Yet never in a spring so compressed.
Something new for us to ponder,
just in case we think we've seen it all.

Old Warrior

Rumpled, crumpled old man
passes my house
on his way to the corner.
Unsteady, weaving zigzags
on short, bowed legs.

Enters my neighbor's
barges right in talking
like he's already at
the Park Joy Bar.

Later, he collapses in my yard.
I worry he's dead
worry my toddlers will see.
Only dead drunk, the police say.
They know him, brush him off
take him to his daughter's
two blocks down.
Not quite right in the head,
one officer tells me.
Shell shock from the war.

Back within hours
he's trying to uproot the stop sign
at Chapel and West Parkway.

It won't budge
but he works at it awhile.
Poor crazed Quixote,
still tilting at the enemy
now a hexagon of red.

Oatmeal

Two cups of water, dash of salt
into the saucepan. Burner on high
cup of rolled oats at the ready—for the boil.
Stir'em in, turn burner low
stir some more and five minutes later
oatmeal for husband and me.

Thirty-five years of oatmeal
in this house on Eton Glen.
Five more, back on West Parkway
where we first worried about cholesterol.
Our parents having died young,
and us, with two toddlers
we couldn't take chances.
So, we went healthy with
those dry, flat, beige, mottled grains
of slightly nutty, slightly cardboardy scent
which cook up into
a beige, slightly nutty, slightly cardboardy-tasting
breakfast—the mushy stuff made by every mom.

Oats, cultivated later than wheat and barley
fed mostly to livestock.
Husked, steamed, rolled and cooked
they're the porridge and gruel given

to orphans, inmates and sailors.
A thickener in haggis, one documentary notes.

Trendy now, oatmeal comes
steel-cut, stone-crushed, pricey
and in Scottish and Irish offerings.
All you need is lots of stuff
to make it, crunchy, flavorful, sweet
interesting and palatable.

Once in Peace Corps days,
a couple of us were making pots of
oatmeal for the hospital in Montero.
Sacks of oats, long lost in storage were found.
On cooking, though, scores of little brown bugs
floated out and up to the surface.
Nothing to do but skim'em off
and throw 'em on the dirt floor.
The chickens would be coming through
soon enough.

I retell this on days I notice
lots of specks in our oatmeal
and husband always says the same thing:
   "Should've left 'em in—more protein."

First Grandchild

Perfect Love sometimes does not come
until the first grandchild.

— Welsh Proverb

I hold him, rocking
rocking in the very chair
in which I rocked his mother.
Vincent looks up.
Six weeks old now.
Slate-grey eyes
beneath a scrunched-up
little-old-man brow.
I stroke his soft, silky
remarkable
full head of black hair,
feel the warmth
of his small body
against my chest.
I am in love
unabashed and unafraid.
For this time
I'm the first time
Grandma.

A New Boy

Godzilla stands proud.
Eighteen inches of
sturdy arms, legs and tail
in dark green plastic.
Plucked from hibernation.
Cleaned and spiffed for re-activation.

Old, in toy monster years
the white slits of his eyes still menace.
And though the spring in his arm
no longer shoots off his hand
and the torn tongue no longer flicks,
he's ready to roll again
on the yellow wheels embedded in his feet.

He remembers his blonde boy.
The laughs, squeals, hugs
play battles and draggings-around.
What a pair they were.
But, now, this new boy, reaching for him
brown-haired, yet familiar of smile
can he measure up?

Dem Bones, Dem Bones
Pre-op thoughts and a song

Sally Field looks good
combating osteoporosis
with her once-a-month pill.
I do fine with a daily dose brand
but while the bone density's better
the arthritis is still worse.
So, months of pain and stumping
around like Walter Brennan
make me look forward to
a knee replacement.

And it comforts me to know
that Neanderthal Man had arthritis, too,
and that they can keep repairing me
joint by joint, this being number three.
More fun at airport security and
more easily identifiable if bones are all that's left.
Best of all, I'll excuse two more pounds as metal.

Yet, I get to thinking sometimes
about what happened to the bone
they cut off my hips. Was it respectful?
Primitive tribes do bad things to each other
when they get hold of rivals' hair,

toenail clippings and bones.
For this surgery, they say
they'll merely "clean up"
around the knee for the implant to fit.
Scraping, smoothing—just dust.
Hope so.

Intrigued by the bones and implants thing,
son-in-law looks up what becomes of them
when you're cremated.
Seems that after you're incinerated
any metal is removed with a magnet
and disposed of in "an approved manner."
Your bones are then ground up and put in the urn.

Too much information, but I'm good to go.
Just wish I could get that darn song out of my head.

Unimagined

I feel good—plate piled high
with quiche, French toast, fresh fruit
and a sticky bun.
Husband and I are at a brunch at church
for folks celebrating their anniversaries.
At our table of three couples,
turns out we're the longest-marrieds
Can't believe it.
Can't believe how old we are.
Used to be, you retired
spent a year or two in the sun, then died.
Folks married forty-five years
were bent, little white-haired people
with canes and old-country accents.

We tablemates take turns
remembering our wedding days:
good weather, bad-in-laws
tight shoes, loose pants
good food, not enough booze
We total up our progeny:
2 kids, 1 grandchild
3 kids, 3 grandchildren
no kids, 1 dog

We tell how we met:
in the neighborhood
at work
through a friend
Not the stuff of great novels.

But it reminds me of what drew
husband and I together
all those years ago
in that bar with a folk singer:
mutual attraction, yes
mutual interests, yes
the feeling it was time, yes
but also the fact that
all of our parents were dead,
none of them making fifty.
Instant empathy and no explaining.
And we never imagined we'd make it this far.

Old Folks in New Tennies

Which creature in the morning goes on four feet,
at noon on two and in the evening upon three?
> — Riddle of the Sphinx

Look out
here we come,
dragging a bit
shuffling
slow
but still upright
and praising the gods
of shoe design
for our roomy-toed
arch-supported
super-cushioned
spring-loaded
Velcro-closing shoes.
Shoes we thank
for keeping us able
to stump the malls
tag along behind grandchildren
shorten our bucket lists
and postpone
that three-legged evening.

III
Others

The Refusal
The passengers of Flight 93

A windswept field
in the highlands
of Pennsylvania
became their grave.
A scraped, scorched
swath of earth with
a mound of fuselage
debris and remains.

They chose that spot.
They chose that hour.

Hijacked, fearful, desperate
in quiet calls they learned
of the Towers and the Pentagon.
Knew they were a missile
pointed at downtown D.C.

Whispering prayers
phoning goodbyes,
they fought—perhaps to live
but at least not to die
taking more innocents with them.

Laugh of the Plesiosaur

Up from the cold and murk
rotating side to side
I rise and break the surface
in the early morning mist,
stretch my slender neck
to the silence all around
then, glide
bisecting the loch
trailing a V-shaped wake.
But only the ruin sees me
the old castle on the hill.
For they are all asleep now
those scientists and film crews
blind to my aqua ballet.
I flex a streamlined flipper
give the water a smack
swirl and paddle
turn and splash
dive deep
confounding their sonar.

Back below, I laugh to think
of their devotion
and their puny proofs.
Carefree, unchangeable
evolutional equal
of the cockroach and the shark
I am amused that
my believers need me so.
They would have invented me
if I did not already exist.
I fire off a torpedo of giggles
to light up and beep their screens.

Anyone But Him

It's not by choice that I,
little brown mare
of chestnut coat
onyx mane and tail
and ink-black legs,
carry this man
this tough-guy tyrant
riding half-naked
for a photo op.
Wish I could tell him
how soft and pasty he looks.
Would if I could
and didn't fear
the gulag
or the glue factory.

The indignity of
this unwanted load.
Wish I were Silver
galloping the West
with the Lone Ranger,
Trigger trotting beneath
a singing Roy,
Bavieca,
steed of the Cid,

carrying the dead champion
into battle one last time.
Love that dead part.
But right now
guess I'd most like to be
the bucking bronco
of Pecos Bill
the one they call
The Widow Maker.

The Death of Shame

I'm dying.
Phased out, cast aside,
dumped by this brazen age.
So rapid my demise
it ought to count as murder.
I hear them chinking out
the inscription on my tombstone now.
ARCHAIC
UNNECESSARY
WE DON'T NEED NO STINKING SHAME NO MORE

Time was I was a somebody,
a cause for fear, remorse
'fessing up, apologizing,
at least a blush.
But now the bad, perverse and cheeky
walk proud, unchallenged.
They get T.V. shows.

Oh, I know, in the past I was invoked
for shunning, honor killings and duels.
all now discredited—and rightly so.
I serve as backup to the Golden Rule.

What a shock, though, to discover
what folks nowadays do—in hopes
it will be done unto them in return.

I fade. Killed, Shameless Ones,
by the unwanted sight of your tattoos,
piercings, cleavages and dirty toenails
the loud-voiced "sharing"
of your cell phone calls
in stores, doctor's offices, lavatory stalls.
Not to mention the media chronicling
of your dysfunctional families,
failed marriages, failed dog-rearing,
failed careers and even your jail time.

Shame on you, I breathe my last.

Drinking Rum Down in the Islands

We watch the ships pass
from our hotel balcony,
so close we hear the music
see the people by the pools
and at the railings waving back.
Floating fiestas the white-tiered
behemoths slipping into
their berths at the pier.
Three in a row
and the one in the middle
able to maneuver
in and out at will.
On island time, we snuggle up
with more Banana Daiquiris
to plan for next year.

I watch again, reclining
drowsy in my chair
downing a Painkiller—not my first.

Splashes and high-pitched calls.
Three huge white whales
breech in the harbor below me,
slapping tails and fins,
landing on their backs
exposing their huge pale bellies
and I swear, laughing.
Crowds line the seawall
to cheer them on
as they head out to sea.

"Come, quick, you've got to see this!"
I yell, but the sentence hangs
echoing weakly into a room as empty
as my empty glass.

Another Llorona

The Weeping Woman of legend haunts the riverbank where she drowned her children, then herself, to spite her unfaithful love.

It was down by the river
that I heard you, Llorona.
On nights I walked sleepless
with a wound that wouldn't heal.
Your cry, piercing, searing
in the howl of the wind
beckoned and I understood,
how first you wept in sorrow
when your love was cast aside,
then, wept in heat and anger
for a vengeance cruel and cold.

I join you, tonight, Llorona,
and I bring my babe,
my sweet, sweet, innocent,
little one I love, even now
as I hold her down.
And when the water takes me, too,
my cries will remain here with yours.

Last Ashfall at Dachau
Arbeit Macht Frei

Final oven firings dust the wrought iron gate,
coat its mocking message a powdery gray.

Work did not make the inmates free.
It was Death
and only now the angels in olive drab
guns slung over their shoulders
like metal wings.

In the town, old Anna cries
for the ash that sometimes dirtied her flowers
for what she didn't ask,
for what she didn't want to know.

No Spring for You
Mother Nature gets menopausal and a bit cranky

How many times have I done this?
And perfectly, too—
the tender chartreuse shoots
the lacy, just-born leaves
the fruit blossom perfume
the creatures stirring
the soil warming.

And yet to such scant praise
and even scanter thanks.
No lack of complaints, though
if the blooms come late
the cold wind lingers
or buds are nipped.
Oaths hurled,
fists clenched
against the sky, then.

Well, Mortals,
I've had enough.
This year
you get no spring—

no tilt toward the sun
no wakening of bears
no muskrats to ramble
no return of the swallows
nor even the turkey buzzards
no flowers
no grass

Just two winters
back to back.

Blue X

In the dust I sweep
from under the refrigerator
an X, a blue plastic magnet
from the set we had when
the kids were young.
Jim and I spelled out words
with the multi-colored alphabet
for the kids to read.
FOX and OX and AX.
A kitchen filled with fun
the X reminds me
and also, he used to smile.

I close my hand
around the magnet
squeeze until it hurts.
We were in love I say,
then slap the magnet back
on the refrigerator door.

Tourist Meets Survivor

Not far below me, at ocean's edge,
an oyster catcher straddles an urchin.
Head bobbing, orange bill stabbing,
it pierces and cracks its prey,
pushes it from my view.
Fascinated, I scramble-slide down the slope
but find only white shell crumbs on dark rock.
Brushing at my scratches, turning to climb back
I nearly step on a black marine iguana
in spiked jurassic skin
and with blunted salt-streaked snout
evolved just for grazing in the sea.
Unhurried, it twitches, tilts its head,
so like a turret with an eye,
which rotating round, judges me
figuring how long I'll stay,
doubting I'll ever adapt.

IV

Nature and Here and There

Intoxication

May moon rises
crisp, pale and full
shines on snow
and white apple blossoms.
Walking my dog
and cursing the chill
I enter a heady perfume.
Inhaling to lungburst
then drunk, craving more
I linger in the orchard
to binge.

Monument Valley

The Creator lingers
in the Valley of the Long Shadows
breath still stirring the wind
warming the sand
ruffling the sage.

Sunset—and the red rocks glow
rosy, incandescent
then a blazing, fiery orange
as lengthening, black shadow fingers
grasp for the valley floor.

Moon rise—and the buttes with fanciful names
Castle, Stagecoach, Bear-and-Rabbit
stand dark in silhouette
profiled against the moon
then bathed in its silvery wash.

Timelessness, awe and beauty
link the ancient ones
the caretakers
the tourists and the movie crews.

Snow Dogies

An unexpected sun
sparkles off icicle-melt
while a playful, street-hugging wind
herds snow swirls down the way.

Late

Thunder rolls,
knocks us from sleep.
Reverberations hang low,
before slowly rumbling away.
Grudging skies weep themselves clean.
By dawn, a long-delayed spring.

A Visit to the Galápagos

I wipe my feet
on a disinfectant-soaked mat,
look up at a mural of an iguana
on the airport wall
and enter the Islas Encantadas.

Amazing, as well as enchanted
these islands spit up from
a hot spot on the ocean floor
like newer, rougher Hawaiis.
Sixteen hundred miles from land
straddling the equator,
buffeted by cold Pacific currents
and the occasional warm El Niño.
Tropical, steaming, barren, baking
inhospitable and beckoning
all at once.

This must be how earth began
how it may end.
Nature's lab, where everything
came by bad luck
dumb luck or serendipity.
Then fought to survive.

We tourists, suffer species envy.
All lotion-slathered, hatted
shod in tough-soled shoes
adapting clumsily to the rafts
the treks on sand, scruff
lava rock and slippery boulders.

But, oh the animals.
One-of-a-kind and unafraid.
Our guide, Renato, coaxes finches
right out of the trees
to come light on his hand.

Black, marine iguanas
who swim like serpents, dive for kelp
and excrete salt from their nostrils
lie so densely-packed, sunning
we have to step around them.

Cormorants who've given up flying
for a duck-like life of bobbing and diving
nest openly and unconcerned
near where they feed.

A female sea lion comes right up
to sniff a tourist's plastic sandal.
Her bull, nearby, bellows, making only
a half-hearted charge, before retreating.

At Darwin Research Station
one big, old, land tortoise raises his head
to let Renato stroke his long, wrinkled neck
as he takes his lettuce treat.
Old friends.
Renato's been feeding him for years.

These giants nearly vanished,
so many taken, for so many years
as food or curiosities.
But with science and nurture and care
They've come back.

All except for Lonesome George,
last great tortoise of his island's kind.
George, who sits alone
while zoos world-wide search for a mate.
Some female taken long ago.
George, who does make stewards of us all.

Hernandez
from Ansel Adams' photo Moonrise

The rising moon
dominates
a darkening sky.

Paler than the stark
cloud layer beneath it
paler than the snow-capped
peaks below.

That moon
smiles down
on a vast, high
arid stretch of plain.
It calms and humbles.

Indifferent,
the desert plants bloom
as they did yesterday
and at the beginning of time.

Scrub trees
mark the stream
that doubtless brought
the mission long ago
later, other buildings
and a utility pole.

The cemetery
houses the few dozen
who passed their lives
nearby.

Hard lives
lived in harsh beauty
but always
so close to heaven
that the moon
knew all their names.

St. Thomas Blues

Blue sky.
Blue sea.
Blue stones
in my new earrings
of the local jewelry.
A contrast to the white
of the clouds
and the sands of the beach.

It's February
and I'm not
in Michigan
anymore.

A breeze,
they say comes
from Portugal,
warms me.
Waves buoy and
splash me
leaving a taste of salt.
I wash that away
with a tropical drink
and feel thankful
to be so blue.

Earotic Sweet Nothings

So soft. So fluffy.
So pink. So white.
So always in the mood.
What do the bunnies whisper
into each other's ears?

Autumn's End

November day
soft, warm and still.
Only yellow, gold
and russet leaves remain.
Translucent, clinging lightly
in the sun.
Until, with slightest rustle
and even slighter sigh
they loosen and let go.

Measurement

At the railing of the Maid of the Mist
I face the thunder of Niagara.
Drenched right through my blue plastic poncho
I dare safely, with fellow tourists
the maelstrom at the bottom of the falls.

The boat bobs and cuts through
the powerful churn and chop.
I look straight up a living wall
its volume so relentless
I'm humbled by the puny
small, endeavors of my life.

Yooper Fungus

There's a fungus among us
in the wilds of the U.P.
It's so old and so enormous
the whole world has come to see.

Fifteen hundred years of living,
forty acres square of spread,
Armillaria Bulbosa,
just your name can summon dread.

And what have you been eating
to sustain your spore field fine?
Do your fungi lie there waiting
for choice snacks on which to dine?

Maybe that's what really happened
to Paul Bunyan and his ox.
Did you snarf them up for breakfast,
just like bagels served with lox?

And maybe that's what happened
to those Indian braves out tracking.
Hiawatha's friends were lost it seems,
but your mushroom lips were smacking.

Did that black robe from St. Ignace
on a shortcut meet his fate?
Did your spongy goo entwine him?
Bit of heaven on your plate?

French traders and fur trappers,
did they turn wrong from Marquette?
It wasn't nice to eat them
while they sang you "Alouette."

Does your mushroom crop sing "Hound Dog"?
Is it wailing "Blue Suede Shoes"?
Did your filaments traverse the Straits
snatching Elvis from Kalamazoo?

Do you sport a union label?
Did you do a shake and shimmy,
when you surely broke the contract rules,
and slithered off with Jimmy?

Oh, Armillaria Bulbosa,
notorious fungus of fame,
When CNN sends out its crews
will you treat them just the same?

Sun Worship

Long days of the solstice
and we bake—willingly
change metabolisms—to bask
as the lizard in us calls.
The sun sets late—reluctant.
We stare in reverence
at the huge, orange, pagan eye.

V
Rants and Rhymes

Bring Back Turbulence

Fasten your seat belts
in case of—
ROUGH AIR.
Yes, I heard it four times
on my last flight.

ROUGH AIR?
Did turbulence have
too many syllables?
Sound too much like
protuberance?
flatulence?
obsolescence?
Did Turbs complain?

ROUGH AIR?
Fasten your seatbelts,
fellow passengers.
There's a dumbed-down,
bumpy language ride ahead.

A Diamond in the Roughage

I shouldn't of et the evidence
that diamond ring I stole.
Now I'm in the clink in trouble
Johnny Law at my toilet bowl.
Yet with push and shout
roughage in roughage out
nuttin' ain't passed yet but time.
Lord, I shouldn't of et that diamond.
Guess thievin's not my line.
And I do repent
know my punishment's
that my ill-gotten gain's now stuck.
And, oh misery, colonoscopy
may be my only luck.
No, I shouldn't of et that piece of ice.
To the straight and narrow I'll bend.
My innards have all been tellin' me
diamonds ain't a gut's best friend.

Coyote Love

I love you Wile E. Coyote
and your never-ending quest
to catch the pesky Road Runner
that "Beep-Beeping," fleet-footed pest.
You fall from buttes and mesas
get squashed 'neath boulders and bricks.
Yet you never lose heart or waver
just come up with more sneaky tricks.
And you always send out to ACME.
You're their customer tried and true.
And they always mail you the latest
in gadgetry phony and new.
And, again the speedster eludes you.
The gimmicks blow up in your face.
But Quixote-like you forge ahead
singed and battered but still in the race.

You Talk Too Much
That 60's song said it all.

Tired, old, attention span short
and shorter.
Tired of listening, masking boredom
and impatience.
So many lectures, rants, sermons
bits of gossip
pearls of medical
and political advice.
Never say much in reply
but that doesn't mean
I want to hear more.
Face betrays me, anyway.

"Just the facts, Ma'am."
Loved that Jack Webb,
love Golden Silence.
Husband hates when
I roll my eyes heavenward
at the start of one of his stories
but I've heard 'em all
so many times
I know 'em better than he does
the truer first versions too.

And now my car gabs
my iPad, my iPhone
even my grill probe.

Hey, are you all talking to ME?
Well, you just talk too much.

Detroit 2009

Hard times,
do not harden my heart.
Today, I am not sorry for
The Man With No Feet.
Today, I feel only
the cold of the pavement,
the cut of the stones.
Today, I need shoes.
And he has none to give.

Bad News Bear

We're discontent,
malcontent,
unemployed
and under stress.
Wall Street sends
no remedy
and Washington
just B.S.

Naked Came the Launderer

*In Michigan, police arrested a college student
for playing the accordion nude in a laundromat.*

In Houghton one midsummer's night
The laundry crowd witnessed a sight.
   An accordionist lewd
   Played a set in the nude.
Some viewed with disgust, some delight.

Night of the Living Pumpkins

They spliced and sliced genetically
those bio-engineers.
And the pumpkin DNA they made
was remarkable—if a bit queer.

Resistant to virus and bruising
its offspring would weigh one ton.
Thus mammoth jack-o-lanterns
could be carved for Halloween fun.

But the scientists were hasty
or perhaps just a little lax,
for into their DNA birthing dish
fell a speck of genetic trash.

Just a bit of Venus Fly Trap
combined with the fledgling veg
adding aggressive tendencies
and a taste for living flesh.

So when this autumn's bounty
ripens in fields and dells,
an orange, carnivorous crop will wait
the pumpkin harvest from Hell.

Crazy for Barney

I spent my Christmas Eve in jail
for maiming a dinosaur.
That jerky, sappy, purple beast
smirked at me in every store.
I couldn't get my shopping done
under his mocking gaze.
He drove me nuts—he was everywhere.
I ended up quite crazed.
He smiled from pillows, bed sheets, games.
My paranoia crept.
I grabbed a popgun and shot that creep
off the toy shelf where he sat.
The shoppers screamed, the clerks did yell.
The guards came in a rush.
Yet, before Security grabbed me,
I drop-kicked that dweeb of plush.
He sailed o'er china, luggage, shoes
and into a live display
of salad shooter veggies
that pock-marked his perky face.
I laughed out loud, and I laughed out long
as they dragged me through the door.
A mother turned psychotic
by a grinning Jurassic bore.

County Pride
Blue Ridge foothills, Virginia

It seems they like
their hard-to-pronounce
if highly suggestive name.
They take their history serious here
figure you should do the same.
But what can you do with a name as bad
as founder FOE-key-ā's?
I try it in French 'cause I can't figure how
to pronounce it another way.
But the locals correct me
not flinching once
for pride of their county dear.
'Cause though anglicized, mangled and naughty
I'm told that—the way to pronounce it's
FAWK-here.

Going Tildeless

A world of print without a tilde
is a sad and wanting place.
We need that squiggly little line
for Spanish letter eñe (N-yea)
A critical diacritical,
a nasalized nyuh, nyuh, nyuh.
Without it there's no mañana
And ene (N-ā) is not enough.

Remember El Niño seasons.
Weather stories every day.
Nary a tilde to be found,
guys called Nino
tired of taking the blame.

But you'd better be even more careful
with a very different pair
año for year and ano for a—h—.
Going tildeless—better not dare.
"All year" must stay todo el año.
and "New Year" stay Año Nuevo.
And although I'll admit
that I have "many years."
Don't you write that as
muchos anos.

Equinoidal

Night equals day and day equals night
at the Equinox it's true.
It's a time for 50-50,
Yin and Yang,
half-and-half to rule.
So, raise your glasses,
half-empty, half-full
and give a half-hearted cheer
for the half-baked, half-crazy
and half-a—d,
who get toasted but twice a year.

Acknowledgements

My thanks to the editors who published these poems—
sometimes in slightly different form than they appear here:

*A Diamond in the Roughage, Anyone But Him, Bad News Bear,
Detroit 2009, Earotic Sweet Nothings, Hernandez, New Mexico,
My Words-in-Waiting, Night of the Living Pumpkins, No Spring for
You, Old Warrior, Intoxication,* and *Sun Worship,* first appeared
in PENINSULA POETS.

Crazy for Barney first appeared in MICHIGAN: LYRICAL
REFLECTIONS OF THE GREAT LAKES.

Fast Times at Euclid Beach first appeared in RIDGEWRITER'S
ANTHOLOGY 2012.

Laugh of the Pleiosaur first appeared in THE MACGUFFIN,
Volume 8.

Yooper Fungus first appeared in THE MATURE AMERICAN.

A special thanks to my publisher and editor, Jeff Caminsky;
to my good friend Lori Goff; to the Ridgewriters of
Farmington Hills, Michigan; to Jonathan Higgins, for
gracing the cover with his beautiful art; and to my teachers
and writing friends at Springfed Arts, Schoolcraft College,
and Oakland County Community College.

About the Author

Ginny Grush lives in Farmington Hills, Michigan with her husband. A former Spanish teacher and Peace Corps volunteer, she has two grown children and one grandchild. She enjoys writing poetry and personal essays, and spoiling her grandson.